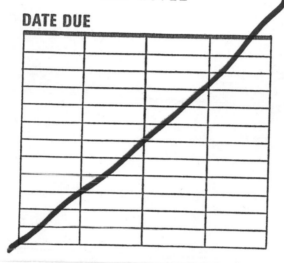

The World, the Flesh

& the Devil

The World, the Flesh & the Devil

AN ENQUIRY INTO THE FUTURE
OF THE THREE ENEMIES OF
THE RATIONAL SOUL

J. D. BERNAL

INDIANA UNIVERSITY PRESS

BLOOMINGTON AND LONDON

FOREWORD

THIS SHORT BOOK WAS THE FIRST I EVER WROTE. I have a great attachment to it because it contains many of the seeds of ideas which I have been elaborating throughout my scientific life. It still seems to me to have validity in its own right.

This essay in prediction was written on the eve of the greatest discoveries and inventions in science. It was written in a world before the discovery of atomic fission—the atom bomb and atomic power; before nuclear fusion and the still distant prospect of unlimited power; in short; before the atomic age.

Some aspects of possible developments of the material world are touched on in the first chapter. Increases in the supply of energy have certainly far exceeded my predictions, hopeful though they were.

Then the next possibility, referred to in the book and now a reality, is the practical achievement of space navigation by rockets—the space age.

There have been two more triumphs in the field of physics, the laser and the electronic computer, the latter now being used in all guidance and communication systems.

Yet, in my opinion, the greatest discovery in all modern science has been one in molecular biology— *the double helix*—which explains in physical, quantum terms, the basis of life and gives some idea of its origin. It is the greatest and most comprehensive idea in all science and, though it may be enlarged and restated, it is unlikely to be radically altered.

The section in the book on the Devil remains the most important but, looking at it now, I find it is expressed too much in Freudian terms which are likely to be superseded. Many new ideas remain just under the horizon, notably those on memory, which now appears to have a chemical basis.

The synthetic chapters at the end of the book need most alteration and real predictive power. Where this might take us, I cannot say. The progress of animal behaviour studies and ethology should help to deduce the future of mankind from its origins.

I have only touched on some of the main new

developments that now have to be taken into account in an attempt to look into our future.

J. D. BERNAL

November 1968

CONTENTS

The World, the Flesh

& the Devil

I

THE FUTURE

THERE ARE TWO FUTURES, THE FUTURE OF DESIRE
and the future of fate, and man's reason has never
learnt to separate them. Desire, the strongest thing
in the world, is itself all future, and it is not for
nothing that in all the religions the motive is always
forwards to an endless futurity of bliss or annihila-
tion. Now that religion gives place to science the
paradisical future of the soul fades before the Utopian future of the species, and still the future rules.
But always there is, on the other side, destiny, that
which inevitably will happen, a future here concerned not as the other was with man and his desires,
but blindly and inexorably with the whole universe
of space and time. The Buddhist seeks to escape
from the Wheel of Life and Death, the Christian

passes through them in the faith of another world to come, the modern reformer, as unrealistic but less imaginative, demands his chosen future in this world of men.

Can we in any better way reconcile desire and fate? In the belief of the scientist the future can yield to an objective analysis only if he can put aside all desire of one future or another; and yet, in reaching for this unattainable understanding, by some mutual influence his desires and the events may grow more and more into harmony. Holding this hope, or better still, moved by a pure curiosity for things to come, how is it possible to examine scientifically the future? For in the science of the future observation is as impossible as experiment; and of the three methods there is left to us only prediction. In the other sciences prediction plays but a small part, and rightly so, for verification follows closely on its heels; but there are general methods in scientific prediction and we may try to apply them in dealing with the whole future state.

First and always, it is necessary to exclude as far as possible, illusion; for to most of us the future is the compensation and fulfilment of all that the present and the past have lacked; and the future being unknown and incontrovertible has been a fair ground on which to place all these hopes and desires. But in

scientific prediction these desires are the most de-
lusive guides. The opposite danger is as great and
more insidious: in our lives we take the present for
granted to an extent far greater than we can realize,
so that even when we are thinking of the future we
cannot separate the historic accidents of the society
in which we were born from the axiomatic bases of
the universe. Until the last few centuries this in-
ability to see the future except as a continuation of
the present prevented any but mystical anticipations
of it. Luckily these complementary errors affect different parts of the future. It is in the near future
where we are still sympathetically related to men
and events that our desires have the most power to
twist our appreciation of facts. We care less about
the more distant future, but to approach it at all we
must divest ourselves of so many customary forms,
that even the more enlightened prophets let their
imagination stop in some static Utopia in despite of
all evidence pointing to ever increasing acceleration
of change.

What positive ideas can be found to take the place
of the naïve anticipation that the future will be like
the present but more pleasant (or more unpleasant
according to one's disposition)? The leading principle is that by which Lyell founded scientific geol-
ogy: the state of the present and the forces operating

in it contain implicitly the future state and point the way to its interpretation. We have three disciplines of thought to help us to this interpretation. History (of which human history is only a minimal part) tells us how things have changed and how by inference they will change in the future. Strictly, prophecy should be treated as part of history, but, until history has found its laws, it must chiefly be used as a storehouse of illustrative facts; though one might say loosely that everything that will happen must conform with the spirit of History. The physical sciences, as far as we know them, give us the material of which future as much as past is built, and the manner of that building. The manner appears to us as physical law but it may well be found to be a tautology which we are congenitally too limited to grasp. Lastly there is the knowledge of our desires, but though the future according to our desires, is an illusion, our desires are, paradoxically, already tending to be the chief agent of change in the universe; it is only that the actual change is so rarely the desired change.

The initial difficulty in the general prediction of the future is its enormous complexity and the interdependence of all its parts; but this complexity is not completely chaotic and we can always attack it by considering it as a product of chance and determinism, chance where we cannot see relationships, determinism where we can. The events out of which so complicated a thing as the general state of the universe is built, form neither one indivisible whole nor a set of equally independent units, but consist of complexes (nebula, planet, sea, animal, society) of which the components are themselves complex parts. This hierarchy of complexes is not imagined to have any objective validity, it is only an expression of the modes of human thought, a convenient simplification which makes science possible. Inside each complex, development proceeds according to its own rules, determined by the nature of the complex; but these rules always include, if they do not entirely reduce to, what is, in effect, the statistical chance interaction of complexes of a lower order. The death-rate of a town, for instance, can be shown to be a function of the amount of money it spends on sanitary measures, but the individual deaths appear, from the point of view of the town, to be due to chance circumstances, though again for each individual concerned they are determined. We can always leave out the higher complexes when we are considering the lower. An atom of oxygen will respond to its environment in the same way in a nebula, in a rock or in the human brain.

Now the complex we are concerned with here is

the human mind, and so we can fairly start with the assumption that the rest of the universe goes on its way determined by its physical, chemical and biological laws except in so far as man himself intervenes. Absolutely, we know hardly anything of these laws, but relatively to our knowledge of human behaviour we know them so well that the future they present— the astronomical, geological, biological future— seems a fixed and stable thing.

In human affairs the immediate future reveals itself in the following of tendencies visible in the present; beyond that must come the application and development of present knowledge. This is the minimal basis for prediction; but our present knowledge carries with it the implication of still further advances in knowledge along the same lines. It is the applications of this new knowledge and the secondary results that flow from them that will chiefly concern us, because it is clearly impossible to go further and include unimagined discovery. Of course, there is a considerable chance that one of the unpredictable discoveries will be so important that it will turn aside the whole course of development. But to be deterred by this chance would be to abandon any attempt at prediction. Already the chance element comes in when we consider applications or developments of knowledge in more than one restricted field; because although we can predict the development in that field fairly well, we cannot predict the rate of development; and so the rates of development in different fields, which are constantly reacting on each other, being unpredictable, the resultant future becomes more and more uncertain the farther we look forward. The only way to deal with this complexity is by separating the variables as best we can, by arbitrarily considering developments as proceeding in one field without any developments in any of the others, and then combining the results attained by applying this method in different fields. At the same time we must keep in mind that the state of development at any one period must be a self-consistent whole. Each line of development must have reached the level which is implied by the necessities of any of the other lines: for instance, the chemical control of life requires the development of chemical technique and apparatus of a very high order. On the other hand, whole sections of certain developments may become superfluous owing to developments in other fields; for instance, the manufacture of synthetic food and the industry connected with it would be unnecessary if blood were used directly as the motive power for animals.

Obviously we cannot proceed with this method in detail: if we could, we should not only be able to predict the future exactly, but to make it the present. For brevity, it is worth considering three fields only.

Man is occupied and has been persistently occupied since his separate evolution, with three kinds of struggle: first with the massive, unintelligent forces of nature, heat and cold, winds, rivers, matter and energy; secondly, with the things closer to him, animals and plants, his own body, its health and disease; and lastly, with his desires and fears, his imaginations and stupidities. In each of these divisions in turn we will make the arbitrary assumption that his progress in it will continue while in other respects he remains the same.

I I

THE WORLD

First, then, in the material world. here pre-diction is on its surest ground, and is, in the first stages, almost a business of mathematics. The physical discoveries of the last twenty-five years must find their application in the world of action—a process which has hardly begun, but the nature of which can easily be seen. So far we have been living on the discoveries of the early and mid-nineteenth century, a macro-mechanical age of power and metal. Essentially it succeeded in substituting mechanism for some of the simpler mechanical movements of the human body, with steam and later electrical power in the place of muscle energy. This was sufficient to revolutionize the whole of human life and to turn the balance definitely for man against the gross natural forces; but the discoveries of the twentieth century, particularly the micro-mechanics of the Quantum Theory which touch on the nature of matter itself, are far more fundamental and must in time produce far more important results. The first step will be the development of new materials and new processes in which physics, chemistry and mechanics will be inextricably fused. The stage should soon be reached when materials can be produced which are not merely modifications of what nature has given us in the way of stones, metals, woods and fibres, but are made to specifications of a molecular architecture. Already we know all the varieties of atoms; we are beginning to know the forces that bind them together; soon we shall be doing this in a way to suit our own purposes. In fact, Professor Goldschmidt of Oslo has already made many model structures in which existing substances are closely copied in different atoms, so as to make a new substance, softer or harder, or more or less fusible. Sulpho-nitrides with silicate structures will be harder and more infusible than anything on earth. A similar substance —carboloy—which is already on the market—combines the strength of steel with the hardness of diamond, and is capable of working glass like a metal. There are similar possible model structures for organic substances; the complexities are greater but the results will be more far-reaching. The linked molecules that make fibres and elastic substances such as rubber or muscle, are already yielding to X-ray investigation; the proteid bodies of living matter must have an analogous but more complex structure. After the analysis will come the synthesis; and for one place in which we can imitate nature we will be able to improve on her in ten, and furnish models of organic materials with more varied properties and capable of withstanding more rigorous conditions. The result—not so very distant—will probably be the passing of the age of metals and all that it implies—mines, furnaces and engines of massive construction. Instead we should have a world of fabric materials, light and elastic, strong only for the purposes for which they are being used, a world which will imitate the balanced perfection of a living body.

At the same time, much that we require for the purposes of modern life would become no longer necessary. With improved systems of chemical manufacture our food and our clothing will be made with much less expenditure of energy in manufacture and transport. And the development of mechanism will not cease: it should turn into more refined forms— heat-engines capable of working at lower and lower temperature differences, engines of higher and higher speed, electrical machines of high potential and high frequency—and should lead to the solution of two most fundamental problems, the efficient transmission of energy by low frequency (wireless) waves, and the direct utilization of the high frequency (light) waves of the sun. On the chemical side the problem of the production of food under controlled conditions, biochemical and ultimately chemical, should become an accomplished fact. In the new synthetic foods will be combined physiological efficacy and a range of flavour equal to that which nature provides, and exceeding it as taste demands; with a range of texture also, the lack of which so far has been the chief disadvantage of substitute food stuffs. With such a variety of combinations to work on, gastronomy will, for the first time, be able to rank with the other arts.

All these developments would lead to a world incomparably more efficient and richer than the present, capable of supporting a much larger population, secure from want and having ample leisure, but still a world limited in space to the surface of the globe and in time to the caprices of geological epochs. Already ambition is stirring in men to conquer space as they conquered the air, and this ambition—at first fantastic—as time goes on becomes more and more reinforced by necessity. Ultimately it would seem

14 ❦

impossible that it should not be solved. Our opponent is here the simple curvature of space-time—a mere matter of acquiring sufficient acceleration on our own part—which, sooner or later, must be practicable. Even now it is possible to imagine methods of accomplishing it, based on no more knowledge than we already possess. The problem of the conquest of space is one in which all the difficulties are at the beginning. Once the earth's gravitational field is overcome, development must follow with immense rapidity. Without going too closely into the mechanical details, it appears that the most effective method is based on the principle of the rocket, and the difficulty, as it exists, is simply that of projecting the particles, whose recoil is being utilized, with the greatest possible velocity, so as to economize both energy and the amount of matter required for propulsion. Up to the present all forms of rocket depend on the movement of masses of gas in which the individual molecules are moving at high velocities in perfectly random directions, and use is only made of the average velocity in the desired direction. What is wanted in the first place is a form of Maxwell's Demon which will allow only those molecules, whose velocities are high and in the direction opposite to the trajectory of the rocket, to escape. The next difficulty is that to set in motion any large rocket the mass of gas required is of the same order as the weight of the rocket itself, so that it is difficult to imagine how the rocket could contain enough material to maintain its propulsion for any length of time. When the radio-transmission of energy is effected half the difficulty will be removed and the projection may very well ultimately be effected by means of positive rays at high potential. It may be that both the problem of space travel and the ethereal transference of energy have already been solved by Professor Japolsky's magnetofugal waves. These are a type of magnetic vortex ring, propagated through space, which, instead of spreading as ordinary electromagnetic waves, remain concentrated along the axis of propagation. Apart from its mode of projection, the construction of the space vessel offers little difficulty since it is essentially the same problem as that of the submarine. Naturally the first space vessels will be extremely cramped and uncomfortable, but they will be manned only by enthusiasts. The problem of landing on any other planet or of returning to earth is much more difficult, mainly because it requires such a nice control of acceleration. Probably the first journeys will be purely for exploration, without landing, and the travellers, if they return to earth at all, will have to abandon their machine and descend in parachutes.

However it is effected, the first leaving of the earth will have provided us with the means of travelling through space with considerable acceleration and, therefore, the possibility of obtaining great velocities—even if the acceleration can only be maintained for a short time. If the problem of the utilization of solar energy has by that time been solved, the movement of these space vessels can be maintained indefinitely. Failing this, a form of space sailing might be developed which used the repulsive effect of the sun's rays instead of wind. A space vessel spreading its large, metallic wings, acres in extent, to the full, might be blown to the limit of Neptune's orbit. Then, to increase its speed, it would tack, close-hauled, down the gravitational field, spreading full sail again as it rushed past the sun.

So far, those who have considered spatial navigation have regarded it from the point of view of exploration and planetary visitation, but the vast importance of escaping from the earth's gravitational field has been almost entirely overlooked. On earth, even if we should use all the solar energy which we receive, we should still be wasting all but one two-billionths of the energy that the sun gives out. Consequently, when we have learnt to live on this solar energy and also to emancipate ourselves from the earth's surface, the possibilities of the spread of humanity will be multiplied accordingly. We can imagine this occurring in definite stages. When the technicalities of space navigation are fully understood there will, from desire or necessity, come the idea of building a permanent home for men in space. The ease of actual navigation in space together with the difficulties of taking-off from or landing on planets like the earth with considerable gravitational fields will in the first place lead to the necessity for bases for repairs and supplies not involving these difficulties. A damaged space vessel would, for instance, almost be bound to be destroyed in attempting earth landing. At first space navigators, and then scientists whose observations would be best conducted outside the earth, and then finally those who for any reason were dissatisfied with earthly conditions would come to inhabit these bases and found permanent spatial colonies. Even with our present primitive knowledge we can plan out such a celestial station in considerable detail.

Imagine a spherical shell ten miles or so in diameter, made of the lightest materials and mostly hollow; for this purpose the new molecular materials would be admirably suited. Owing to the absence of gravitation its construction would not be an engineering feat of any magnitude. The source of the material out of which this would be made would only be in small part drawn from the earth; for the great bulk of the structure would be made out of the substance of one or more smaller asteroids, rings of Saturn or other planetary detritus. The initial stages of construction are the most difficult to imagine. They will probably consist of attaching an asteroid of some hundred yards or so diameter to a space vessel, hollowing it out and using the removed material to build the first protective shell. Afterwards the shell could be re-worked, bit by bit, using elaborated and more suitable substances and at the same time increasing its size by diminishing its thickness. The globe would fulfil all the functions by which our earth manages to support life. In default of a gravitational field it has, perforce, to keep its atmosphere and the greater portion of its life inside; but as all its nourishment comes in the form of energy through its outer surface it would be forced to resemble on the whole an enormously complicated single-celled plant.

The outermost layer would have a protective and assimilative character. The presence of meteoric matter in the solar system moving at high speeds in eccentric orbits would be the most formidable danger in space travelling and space inhabitation. Certain meteorite swarms could be avoided altogether by keeping out of their tracks; larger meteorites could be detected at a distance by visual observation or by the effect of their gravitational fields. These might be avoided by changing the course of the globe or deflecting the meteorites by firing high-speed projectiles into them. Smaller meteorites would be impossible to avoid. The shell of the globe would have to be made strong enough not to be penetrated or cracked by them, and would have to possess regenerative mechanisms for repairing superficial damage. Possibly the function which our atmosphere performs for the earth could be imitated by jets of high-speed gas or electrons which, projected at meteorites, would vapourize them and thus prevent them doing any damage. At the same time meteoric matter might be the chief source of the material required for the growth or propulsion of the globe if a method of assimilating it could be found.

The outer shell would be hard, transparent and thin. Its chief functions would be to prevent the escape of gases from the interior, to preserve the rigidity of the structure, and to allow the free access of radiant energy. Immediately underneath this epidermis would be the apparatus for utilizing this energy either in the form of a network of vessels carrying a chlorophyll-like fluid capable of re-synthesizing carbohydrate bodies from carbon dioxide, or some purely electrical contrivance for the absorption of radiant energy. In the latter case the globe would almost certainly be supplied with vast, tenuous, membranous wings which would increase its area of utilization of sunlight. The subcutaneous circulation would also have the necessary function of dissipating superfluous heat, in as low temperature radiation as possible. Underneath this layer would probably lie the main stores of the globe in the form of layers of solid oxygen, ice and carbon or hydro-carbons. Inside these layers, which might be a quarter of a mile in thickness, would lie the controlling mechanisms of the globe. These mechanisms would primarily maintain the general metabolism, that is, they would regulate the internal atmosphere and climate both as to composition and movements. They would elaborate the necessary food products and distribute mechanical energy where it was required. They would also deal with all waste matters, reconverting them with the use of energy into a consumable form; for it must be remembered that the globe takes the place of the whole earth and not of any part of it, and in the earth nothing can afford to be permanently wasted. In this layer, too, would be the workshops and laboratories concerned with the improvement of the globe and arrangements for its growth.

Inside the mechanical layer would be the living region and here imagination has a more difficult task. It would, of course, not be necessary to have either houses or rooms in the same sense in which we have them on the earth. The absence of bad weather and of gravitation make most of the uses that we have for houses superfluous. Perhaps we can safely assume that a certain number of cells closed by thin, but sound-proof, partitions would be necessary for work requiring special isolation, but the major part of the lives of the inhabitants of the globe would be spent in the free space which would occupy the greater portion of the centre of the globe.

This three-dimensional, gravitationless way of living is very difficult for us to imagine, but there is no reason to suppose that we would not ultimately adjust ourselves to it. We should be released from the way we are dragged down on the surface of the earth all our lives: the slightest push against a relatively rigid object would send us yards away; a good jump—and we should be spinning across from one side of the globe to the other. Resistanace to the air would, of course, come in, as it does on the earth; but this could be turned to advantage by the use of short wings. Objects would become endowed with a peculiar levity. We should have to devise ways of holding them in place other than by putting them down; liquids and powders would at first cause great complications. An attempt to put down a cup of tea would result in the cup descending and the tea remaining as a vibrating globule in the air. Dust would be an unbearable nuisance and would have to be suppressed, because even wetting it would never make it settle. We should find in the end that all these things were great conveniences, but at first they would be extremely awkward. The possibilities of three-dimensional life would make the globes much roomier than their size would suggest. A globe interior eight miles across would contain as much effective space as a countryside one hundred and fifty miles square even if one gave a liberal allowance of air, say fifty feet above the ground.

The activity of the globe is, of course, by no means confined to its interior. In the first place it would necessarily have a number of effective sense and motor organs. Essentially the former would consist of an observatory which continually recorded the position of the globe and at the same time kept a look-out for any meteoric bodies of perceptible size which might damage it. On the whole the globe would not be designed for travel. It would move in an orbit around the sun without any expenditure of energy; but occasionally it might be necessary to shift its orbital position to a more advantageous one, and for this it would require a small motor of a rocket variety.

Yet the globe would be by no means isolated. It

would be in continuous communication by wireless with other globes and with the earth, and this communication would include the transmission of every sort of sense message which we have at present acquired as well as those which we may require in the future. Interplanetary vessels would insure the transport of men and materials, and see to it that the colonies were not isolated units.

However, the essential positive activity of the globe or colony would be in the development, growth and reproduction of the globe. A globe which was merely a satisfactory way of continuing life indefinitely would barely be more than a reproduction of terrestrial conditions in a more restricted sphere. But the necessity of preserving the outer shell would prevent a continuous alteration of structure, and development would have to proceed either by the crustacean-like development in which a new and better globe could be put together inside the larger one, which could be subsequently broken open and reabsorbed; or, as in the molluscs, by the building out of new sections in a spiral form; or, more probably, by keeping the even simpler form of behaviour of the protozoa by the building of a new globe outside the original globe, but in contact with it until it should be in a position to set up an independent existence.

So far we have considered the construction and mechanism of the globe rather than its inhabitants. The inhabitants can be divided into the personnel or crew, and the citizens or passengers. With the first —except that their tasks would be more complicated and more scientific than those that fall to the officers and crew of a modern ship—we need not be concerned. To the others the globes would appear both as hotels and laboratories. The population of each globe would be by no means fixed; constant interchange would be taking place between them and the earth even when the greater portion of human beings were actually inhabiting globes. There would probably be no more need for government than in a modern hotel: there would be a few restrictions concerned with the safety of the vessel and that would be all.

Criticism might be made on the ground that life in a globe, say of twenty or thirty thousand inhabitants would be extremely dull, and that the diversity of scene, of animals and plants and historical associations which exist even in the smallest and most isolated country on the earth would be lacking. This criticism is valid on the initial assumption that men have not in any way changed. Here, to make globe life plausible, we must anticipate the later chapters and assume men's interests and occupations to have altered. Already the scientist is more immersed in his work and concentrates more on relations with his colleagues than in the immediate life of his neighbourhood. On the other hand, present æsthetic tendencies verge towards the abstract and do not demand so much inspiration from untouched nature. What has made a small town or a small country seem in the past a narrow sphere of interest has been on the one hand its isolation, and on the other hand the fact that the majority of its inhabitants are at so low a level of culture as to prevent any considerable intellectual interchange within its boundaries. Neither limitation holds for the globes, and the case of ancient Athens is enough to show that small size alone does not prevent cultural activity. Free communications and voluntary associations of interested persons will be the rule, and for those whose primary interest is in primitive nature there will always remain the earth which, free from the economic necessity of producing vast quantities of agricultural products, could be allowed to revert to a very much more natural state.

As the globes multiplied they would undoubtedly develop very differently according to their construction and to the tendencies of their colonies, and at the same time they would compete increasingly both for the sunlight which kept them alive and for the asteroidal and meteoric matter which enabled them to grow. Sooner or later this pressure, or perhaps the knowledge of the imminent failure of the sun, would force some more adventurous colony to set out beyond the bounds of the solar system. The difficulty involved in making this jump is probably as great as that of leaving the earth itself. Interstellar distances are so large that high velocities, approaching those of light, would be necessary; and though high velocities would be easy to attain—it being merely a matter of allowing acceleration to accumulate—they would expose the space vessels to very serious dangers, particularly from dispersed meteoric bodies. A space vessel would, in fact, have to be a comet, ejecting from its anterior end a stream of gas which, meeting and vapourizing any matter in its path, would sweep it to the sides and behind in a luminous trail. Such a method would be very wasteful of matter, and one might perhaps count on some better one having been devised by that time. Even with such velocities journeys would have to last for hundreds and thousands of years, and it would be necessary—if man remains as he is—for colonies of ancestors to start out who might expect the arrival of remote descendants. This would require a self-sacrifice and a perfection of educational method that we could hardly demand at the present. However, once acclimatized to space living, it is unlikely that man will stop until he has roamed over and colonized most of the sidereal universe, or that even this will be the end. Man will not ultimately be content to be parasitic on the stars but will invade them and organize them for his own purposes.

A star is essentially an immense reservoir of energy which is being dissipated as rapidly as its bulk will allow. It may be that, in the future, man will have no use for energy and be indifferent to stars except as spectacles, but if (and this seems more probable) energy is still needed, the stars cannot be allowed to continue in their old way, but will be turned into efficient heat engines. The second law of thermodynamics which, as Jeans delights in pointing out to us, will ultimately bring this universe to an inglorious close, may perhaps always remain the final factor. But by intelligent organization the life of the universe could probably be prolonged to many millions of millions of times what it would be without organization. Besides, we are still too close to the birth of the universe to be certain about its death. In any case, long before these questions become urgent it would seem impossible not to assume that man himself would have changed radically in this environment and the nature of this change we must consider in the next chapter.

I I I

THE FLESH

In the alteration of himself man has a great deal further to go than in the alteration of his inorganic environment. He has been doing the latter more or less unconsciously and empirically for several thousand years, ever since he ceased being parasitic on his environment like any other animal, and consciously and intelligently for at least hundreds of years; whereas he has not been able to change himself at all and has had only fifty years or so to begin to understand how he works. Of course, this is not strictly true: man has altered himself in the evolutionary process, he has lost a good deal of hair, his wisdom teeth are failing to pierce, and his nasal passages are becoming more and more degenerate. But the processes of natural evolution are so much slower than the development of man's control over environment that we might, in such a developing world, still consider man's body as constant and unchanging. If it is not to be so then man himself must actively interfere in his own making and interfere in a highly unnatural manner. The eugenists and apostles of healthy life, may, in a very considerable course of time, realize the full potentialities of the species: we may count on beautiful, healthy and long-lived men and women, but they do not touch the alterations of the species. To do this we must alter either the germ plasm or the living structure of the body, or both together. The first method—the favourite of Mr. J. B. S. Haldane—has so far received most attention. With it we might achieve such a variation as we have empirically produced in dogs and goldfish, or perhaps even manage to produce new species with special potentialities. But the method is bound to be slow and finally limited by the possibilities of flesh and blood. The germ plasm is a very inaccessible unit, before we can deal with it adequately we must isolate it, and to do this already involves us in surgery. It is quite conceivable that the mechanism of evolution, as we know it up to the present, may well be superseded at this point. Biologists are apt, even if they are not vitalists, to consider it as almost divine; but after all it is only nature's way of achieving a shifting equilibrium with an environment; and if we can find a more direct way by the use of intelligence, that way is bound to supersede the unconscious mechanism of growth and reproduction.

In a sense we have already started using the direct method; when the ape-ancestor first used a stone he was modifying his bodily structure by the inclusion of a foreign substance. This inclusion was temporary, but with the adoption of clothes there began a series of permanent additions to the body, affecting nearly all its functions and even, as with spectacles, its sense organs. In the modern world, the variety of objects which really form part of an effective human body is very great. Yet they all (if we except such rarities as artificial larynges) still have the quality of being outside the cell layers of the human body. The decisive step will come when we extend the foreign body into the actual structure of living matter. Parallel with this development is the alteration of the body by tampering with its chemical reactions—again a very old-established but rather sporadic process resorted to to cure illness or procure intoxication. But with the development of surgery on the one hand and physiological chemistry on the other, the possibility of radical alteration of the body appears for the first time. Here we may proceed, not by allowing evolution to work the changes, but by copying and short-circuiting its methods.

The changes that evolution produces apart from mere growth in size, or diversity of form without change of function, are in the nature of perversions: a part of the fish's gut becomes a swimming bladder, the swimming bladder becomes the lung; a salivary gland and an extra eye are charged with the function of producing hormones. Under the pressure of environment or whatever else is the cause of evolution, nature takes hold of what already had existed for some now superseded activity, and with a minimum of alteration gives it a new function. There is nothing essentially mysterious in the process: it is both the easiest and the only possible way of achieving the change. Starting *de novo* to deal with a new situation is not within the power of natural, unintelligent processes; they can only modify in a limited way already existing structures by altering their chemical environment. Men may well copy the process, in so far as original structures are used as the basis for new ones, simply because this is the most economical method, but they are not bound to the very limited range of methods of change which nature adopts.

Now modern mechanical and modern chemical discoveries have rendered both the skeletal and metabolic functions of the body to a large extent useless.

In teleological biochemistry one might say that an animal moves his limbs in order to get his food, and uses his body organs in order to turn that food into blood to keep his body alive and active. Now if man is only an animal this is all very satisfactory, but viewed from the standpoint of the mental activity by which he increasingly lives, it is a highly inefficient way of keeping his mind working. In a civilized worker the limbs are mere parasites, demanding nine-tenths of the energy of the food and even a kind of blackmail in the exercise they need to prevent disease, while the body organs wear themselves out in supplying their requirements. On the other hand, the increasing complexity of man's existence, particularly the mental capacity required to deal with its mechanical and physical complications, gives rise to the need for a much more complex sensory and motor organization, and even more fundamentally for a better organized cerebral mechanism. Sooner or later the useless parts of the body must be given more modern functions or dispensed with altogether, and in their place we must incorporate in the effective body the mechanisms of the new functions. Surgery and biochemistry are sciences still too young to predict exactly how this will happen. The account I am about to give must be taken rather as a fable.

Take, as a starting point, the perfect man such

as the doctors, the eugenists and the public health officers between them hope to make of humanity: a man living perhaps an average of a hundred and twenty years but still mortal, and increasingly feeling the burden of this mortality. Already Shaw in his mystical fashion cries out for life to give us hundreds of years to experience, learn and understand; but without the vitalist's faith in the efficacy of human will we shall have to resort to some artifice to achieve this purpose. Sooner or later some eminent physiologist will have his neck broken in a super-civilized accident or find his body cells worn beyond capacity for repair. He will then be forced to decide whether to abandon his body or his life. After all it is brain that counts, and to have a brain suffused by fresh and correctly prescribed blood is to be alive—to think. The experiment is not impossible; it has already been performed on a dog and that is three-quarters of the way towards achieving it with a human subject. But only a Brahmin philosopher would care to exist as an isolated brain, perpetually centred on its own meditations. Permanently to break off all communications with the world is as good as to be dead. However, the channels of communication are ready to hand. Already we know the essential electrical nature of nerve impulses; it is a matter of delicate surgery to attach nerves permanently to apparatus which will either send messages to the nerves or receive them. And the brain thus connected up continues an existence, purely mental and with very different delights from those of the body, but even now perhaps preferable to complete extinction. The example may have been too far-fetched; perhaps the same result may be achieved much more gradually by using of the many superfluous nerves with which our body is endowed for various auxiliary and motor services. We badly need a small sense organ for detecting wireless frequencies, eyes for infra-red, ultra-violet and X-rays, ears for supersonics, detectors of high and low temperatures, of electrical potential and current, and chemical organs of many kinds. We may perhaps be able to train a great number of hot and cold and pain receiving nerves to take over these functions; on the motor side we shall soon be, if we are not already, obliged to control mechanisms for which two hands and feet are an entirely inadequate number; and, apart from that, the direction of mechanism by pure volition would enormously simplify its operation. Where the motor mechanism is not primarily electrical, it might be simpler and more effective to use nerve-muscle preparations instead of direct nerve connections. Even the pain nerves may be pressed into service to report any failure in the associated mechanism. A mechanical stage, utilizing some or all of these alterations of the bodily frame might, if the initial experiments were successful in the sense of leading to a tolerable existence, become the regular culmination to ordinary life. Whether this should ever be so for the whole of the population we will discuss later, but for the moment we may attempt to picture what would at this period be the course of existence for a transformable human being.

Starting, as Mr. J. B. S. Haldane so convincingly predicts, in an ectogenetic factory, man will have anything from sixty to a hundred and twenty years of larval, unspecialized existence—surely enough to satisfy the advocates of the natural life. In this stage he need not be cursed by the age of science and mechanism, but can occupy his time (without the conscience of wasting it) in dancing, poetry and love-making, and perhaps incidentally take part in the reproductive activity. Then he will leave the body whose potentialities he should have sufficiently explored.

The next stage might be compared to that of a chrysalis, a complicated and rather unpleasant process of transforming the already existing organs and grafting on all the new sensory and motor mechanisms. There would follow a period of re-education in which he would grow to understand the functioning of his new sensory organs and practise the manipulation of his new motor mechanism. Finally, he would emerge as a completely effective, mentally-directed mechanism, and set about the tasks appropriate to his new capacities. But this is by no means the end of his development, although it marks his last great metamorphosis. Apart from such mental development as his increased faculties will demand from him, he will be physically plastic in a way quite transcending the capacities of untransformed humanity. Should he need a new sense organ or have a new mechanism to operate, he will have undifferentiated nerve connections to attach to them, and will be able to extend indefinitely his possible sensations and actions by using successively different end-organs.

The carrying out of these complicated surgical and physiological operations would be in the hands of a medical profession which would be bound to come rapidly under the control of transformed men. The operations themselves would probably be conducted by mechanisms controlled by the transformed heads of the profession, though in the earlier and experimental stages, of course, it would still be done by human surgeons and physiologists.

It is much more difficult to form a picture of the final state, partly because this final state would be so fluid and so liable to improve, and partly because there would be no reason whatever why all people should transform in the same way. Probably a great number of typical forms would be developed, each specialized in certain directions. If we confine ourselves to what might be called the first stage of mechanized humanity and to a person mechanized for scientific rather than æsthetic purposes—for to predict even the shapes that men would adopt if they would make of *themselves* a harmony of form and sensation must be beyond imagination—then the description might run roughly as follows.

Instead of the present body structure we should have the whole framework of some very rigid material, probably not metal but one of the new fibrous substances. In shape it might well be rather a short cylinder. Inside the cylinder, and supported very carefully to prevent shock, is the brain with its nerve connections, immersed in a liquid of the nature of cerebro-spinal fluid, kept circulating over it at a uniform temperature. The brain and nerve cells are kept supplied with fresh oxygenated blood and drained off de-oxygenated blood through their arteries and veins which connect outside the cylinder to the artificial heart-lung digestive system—an elaborate, automatic contrivance. This might in large part be made from living organs, although these would have to be carefully arranged so that no failure on their part would

endanger the blood supply to the brain (only a frac-
tion of the body's present requirements) and so that
they could be inter-changed and repaired without dis-
turbing its functions. The brain thus guaranteed continuous awareness, is connected in the anterior of the
case with its immediate sense organs, the eye and
the ear—which will probably retain this connection
for a long time. The eyes will look into a kind of op-
tical box which will enable them alternatively to look
into periscopes projecting from the case, telescopes,
microscopes and a whole range of televisual apparatus. The ear would have the corresponding micro-
phone attachments and would still be the chief organ
for wireless reception. Smell and taste organs, on
the other hand, would be prolonged into connections
outside the case and would be changed into chemical
testing organs, achieving a more conscious and less
primitively emotional role than they have at present.
It may perhaps be impossible to do this owing to the
peculiarly close relation between the brain and olfac-
tory organs, in which case the chemical sense would
have to be indirect. The remaining sensory nerves,
those of touch, temperature, muscular position and
visceral functioning, would go to the corresponding
part of the exterior machinery or to the blood supplying organs. Attached to the brain cylinder would be
its immediate motor organs, corresponding to but

much more complex than, our mouth, tongue and hands. This appendage system would probably be built up like that of a crustacean which uses the same general type of arm for antenna, jaw and limb; and they would range from delicate micro-manipulators to levers capable of exerting considerable forces, all controlled by the appropriate motor nerves. Closely associated with the brain-case would also be sound, colour and wireless producing organs. In addition to these there would be certain organs of a type we do not possess at present—the self-repairing organs—which under the control of the brain would be able to manipulate the other organs, particularly the visceral blood supply organs, and to keep them in effective working order. Serious derangements, such as those involving loss of consciousness would still, of course, call for outside assistance, but with proper care these would be in the nature of rare accidents.

The remaining organs would have a more temporary connection with the brain-case. There would be locomotor apparatus of different kinds, which could be used alternatively for slow movement, equivalent to walking, for rapid transit and for flight. On the whole, however, the locomotor organs would not be much used because the extension of the sense organs would tend to take their place. Most of these would be mere mechanisms quite apart from the body; there would be the sending parts of the television apparatus, tele-acoustic and tele-chemical organs, and tele-sensory organs of the nature of touch for determining all forms of texture. Besides these there would be various tele-motor organs for manipulating materials at great distances from the controlling mind. These extended organs would only belong in a loose sense to any particular person, or rather, they would belong only temporarily to the person who was using them and could equivalently be operated by other people. This capacity for indefinite extension might in the end lead to the relative fixity of the different brains; and this would, in itself, be an advantage from the point of view of security and uniformity of conditions, only some of the more active considering it necessary to be on the spot to observe and do things.

The new man must appear to those who have not contemplated him before as a strange, monstrous and inhuman creature, but he is only the logical outcome of the type of humanity that exists at present. It may be argued that this tampering with bodily mechanism is as unnecessary as it is difficult, that all the increase of control needed may be obtained by extremely responsive mechanisms outside the unaltered human body. But though it is possible that in the early stages a surgically transformed man would actually be at a disadvantage in capacity of perform-ance to a normal, healthy man, he would still be better off than a dead man. Although it is possible that man has far to go before his inherent physiolog-ical and psychological make-up becomes the limiting factor to his development, this must happen sooner or later, and it is then that the mechanized man will begin to show a definite advantage. Normal man is an evolutionary dead end; mechanical man, appar-ently a break in organic evolution, is actually more in the true tradition of a further evolution.

A much more fundamental break is implicit in the means of his development. If a method has been found of connecting a nerve ending in a brain di-rectly with an electrical reactor, then the way is open for connecting it with a brain-cell of another person. Such a connection being, of course, essentially elec-trical, could be effected just as well through the ether as along wires. At first this would limit itself to the more perfect and economic transference of thought which would be necessary in the co-operative thinking of the future. But it cannot stop here. Con-nections between two or more minds would tend to become a more and more permanent condition until they functioned as dual or multiple organisms. The minds would always preserve a certain individuality, the network of cells inside a single brain being more dense than that existing between brains, each brain being chiefly occupied with its individual mental development and only communicating with the others for some common purpose. Once the more or less permanent compound brain came into existence two of the ineluctable limitations of present existence would be surmounted. In the first place death would take on a different and far less terrible aspect. Death would still exist for the mentally-directed mechanism we have just desscribed; it would merely be postponed for three hundred or perhaps a thousand years, as long as the brain cells could be persuaded to live in the most favourable environment, but not for ever. But the multiple individual would be, barring cataclysmic accidents, immortal, the older components as they died being replaced by newer ones without losing the continuity of the self, the memories and feelings of the older member transferring themselves almost completely to the common stock before its death. And if this seems only a way of cheating death, we must realize that the individual brain will feel itself part of the whole in a way that completely transcends the devotion of the most fanatical adherent of a religious sect. It is admittedly difficult to imagine this state of affairs effectively. It would be a state of ecstasy in the literal sense, and this is the second great alteration that the compound mind makes possible. Whatever the intensity of our feeling, however much we may strive to reach beyond ourselves or into another's mind, we are always barred by the limitations of our individuality. Here at least those barriers would be down: feeling would truly communicate itself, memories would be held in common, and yet in all this, identity and continuity of individual development would not be lost. It is possible, even probable, that the different individuals of a compound mind would not all have similar functions or even be of the same rank of importance. Division of labour would soon set in: to some minds might be delegated the task of ensuring the proper functioning of the others, some might specialize in sense reception and so on. Thus would grow up a hierarchy of minds that would be more truly a complex than a compound mind.

The complex minds could, with their lease of life, extend their perceptions and understanding and their actions far beyond those of the individual. Time senses could be altered: the events that moved with the slowness of geological ages would be apprehended as movement, and at the same time the most rapid vibrations of the physical world could be separated. As we have seen, sense organs would tend to be less and less attached to bodies, and the host of subsidiary, purely mechanical agents and perceptors would be capable of penetrating those regions where organic bodies cannot enter or hope to survive. The interior of the earth and the stars, the inmost cells of living things themselves, would be open to consciousness through these angels, and through these angels also the motions of stars and living things could be directed.

This is perhaps far enough; beyond that the future must direct itself. Yet why should we stop until our imaginations are exhausted. Even beyond this there are foreseeable possibilities. Undoubtedly the nature of life processes themselves will be far more intensively studied. To make life itself will be only a preliminary stage, because in its simplest phases life can differ very little from the inorganic world. But the mere making of life would only be important if we intended to allow it to evolve of itself anew. This, as Mr. Whyte suggests in *Archimedes*, is necessarily a lengthy process, but there is no need to wait for it. Instead, artificial life would undoubtedly be used as ancillary to human activity and not allowed to evolve freely except for experimental purposes. Men will not be content to manufacture life: they will want to improve on it. For one material out of which nature has been forced to make life, man will have a thousand; living and organized material will be as much at the call of the mechanized or compound man as metals are to-day, and gradually this living material will come to substitute more and more for such inferior functions of the brain as memory, reflex actions, etc., in the compound man himself; for bodies at this time would be left far behind. The brain itself would become more and more separated into different groups of cells or individual cells with complicated connections, and probably occupying considerable space. This would mean loss of motility which would not be a disadvantage owing to the extension of the sense faculties. Every part would not be accessible for replacing or repairing and this would in itself ensure a practical eternity of existence, for even the replacement of a previously organic brain-cell by a synthetic apparatus would not destroy the continuity of consciousness.

The new life would be more plastic, more directly controllable and at the same time more variable and more permanent than that produced by the triumphant opportunism of nature. Bit by bit the heritage in the direct line of mankind—the heritage of the original life emerging on the face of the world —would dwindle, and in the end disappear effectively, being preserved perhaps as some curious relic, while the new life which conserves none of the substance and all the spirit of the old would take its place and continue its development. Such a change would be as important as that in which life first appeared on the earth's surface and might be as gradual and imperceptible. Finally, consciousness itself may end or vanish in a humanity that has become completely etherialized, losing the close-knit organism, becoming masses of atoms in space communicating by radiation, and ultimately perhaps resolving itself entirely into light. That may be an end or a beginning, but from here it is out of sight.

I V

THE DEVIL

WHY DO THE FIRST LINES OF ATTACK AGAINST the inorganic forces of the world and the organic structure of our bodies seem so doubtful, fanciful and Utopian? Because we can abandon the world and subdue the flesh only if we first expel the devil, and the devil, for all that he has lost individuality, is still as powerful as ever. The devil is the most difficult of all to deal with: he is inside ourselves, we cannot see him. Our capacities, our desires, our inner confusions are almost impossible to understand or cope with in the present, still less can we predict what will be the future of them. Psychology at the present day is hardly in a better state than physics in the time of Aristotle; it has acquired a vocabulary, the general movements and transformations of con-

scious and unconscious motives are described, but
nothing more. Yet in the absence of scientific analysis
something must be said, because all the changes I
have predicted in the organic or inorganic world
must, in the first place, start from some human psychological motive and effect themselves through the
operation of human intellectual processes. We are
obviously not in a position to predict the particular
new orientations which a change in psychology
would give to human development, beyond that
which would result from the removal of what we
know are inhibitory causes, so that here I will only
attempt to estimate the effect of psychological forces
in preventing or retarding the kind of processes outlined in the first two sections. The progress of the
future depends no longer on physiological evolution
but on the reaction of intelligence on a material universe. It will be hindered or stopped either by a failure in the capacity for maintaining creative intellectual thinking, or by the lack of desire to apply such
thinking to the progress of humanity, or, of course,
by both these causes together. Consider first the retarding factors that endanger the capacity for creative thinking. Some are apparent now. It is pretty
clear that they are ineffective in stopping the course
of thought at present, but they have not always been
so in the past and we cannot be sure that they will

not be so in the future. One of the most threatening retarding factors of the present is specialization, particularly as it is bound to increase with scientific knowledge itself. But it is doubtful whether specialization in itself is capable of bringing scientific thought to a standstill. It retards it in so far as the specialist is ignorant of current thought in other fields, and the remedy for this is obviously an intelligently operated system of distribution and grading of knowledge so that each worker may have the amount that he requires outside his own field, in a form which can be absorbed with a minimum of mental effort. The problem is essentially that of communications to an army in action. After a rapid advance communications become disorganized, and there is a temporary halting until they are again in working order.

Such an organization of intellectual work for definite ends involves a fundamental change: it is analogous to the change from a food-gathering to a food-producing society. The modern scientist is a primitive savage. If he is active and enterprising he tracks his prey down alone or in small parties; if he is industrious and thorough he gathers and piles up the natural products around him, but for his success he has to thank not only his own skill and the lore of his craft, but the richness of nature and the paucity of his companions. Good hunting will not last much longer, but the tilled ground is richer.

We shall be forced to attempt planned and directed researchers employing hundreds of workers for many years, and this cannot be done without risking the loss of independence and originality. This is a serious and fundamental obstacle but it may be overcome in two ways. It should be possible so to improve educational methods, that mental activity, the capacity to form new associations, should not be incompatible with the performance of routine work: that is, every research worker should be potentially able to add to and modify the whole course of the research and suggestions. At the same time it is certain that originality, organizing power and industri-ousness will continue as now to be very unevenly distributed; and it is an essentially social problem to make the best apportionment of functions, using for the more routine operations people who under present conditions would not be scientific workers at all, and using the organizers to translate into plans of action the incoherent ideas of the thinkers. Pedantry and bureaucracy—symptoms of an unintelligent respect for the past—are at present real dangers, but, once their genesis is understood, they can be made to vanish.

Specialization is brought about by the wideness

of the field in which science operates, but as we go more deeply into nature the intrinsic complication of the phenomena increases and the modes of thinking used in ordinary life become more inadequate to deal with them. It is conceivable that the supply of minds capable of making any impression on these deeper problems may more and more fall behind the number required, and that all the efforts of education to produce ten genii where one grew before will be foiled by intrinsic difficulties in nature. It is impossible to know whether this will happen. One may guess, from experience of the past, that nature is never so complicated as it looks; that the value of theory and deductive thinking and the use of appropriate language and symbolism will reduce the difficulties in the measure that they are approached.

However they appear to the pessimist of the present day, it is not in specialization or complication that the chief danger to progress seems to lie: it is in something much more deep-seated and much more elusive. Bertrand Russell, in one of his "Sceptical Essays," predicting the approaching end of the scientific age, suggests that people will turn from physics to metaphysics because the hope that the former held out is seen to be vain except to new, half-cultivated peoples. Perhaps after all it is hope that really determines whether an age is or is not creative. But the existence of hope in a society at any time itself depends on many unexplored psychological, economic and political causes. I do not think that the factors involved are of a mystical order, but that they require considerable disentangling.

There seem to be two psychological determinants in any culture: a crop of perverted individuals capable of more than average performance, and a mass of people effective not so much by their number as by their secure hold on tradition. In the normal state the perverse are dominated by the mass in two ways. Their mode of expression is dictated by the modes conceivable in the society; everywhere, even the most aberrant individual must conform to one of a small number of recognized types. The same type of mind that would now make a physicist would in the middle ages have made a scholastic theologian. Further, there is a process of selection in which the current tradition decides what is to be the relative value and effectiveness of each type. Thus, even, if at all times types are always produced in the same abundance, only the selected are effective, as meditative ascetics in India or energetic salesmen in America. The mass of the people, or more properly the ruling class, pay the piper and they call the tune; genius is potent only when it fits the tendencies of the age. From this standpoint we are approaching the close of the period of respectable comfort which puritanism demanded and mathematics and handicraft produced. But this period may not end in a regression to the mediæval state through the ultimate dissatisfaction with science; before that happens science, raised to power by industrialism, may in its turn become the directing tradition.

Political and social events must also be effective, but not in a very obvious fashion. Both political confusion and prolonged peace undoubtedly affect creative thought but whether they respectively hinder or help it is not at all certain. When one contrasts Athens, renaissance Italy and feudal China, on the one hand, with the Roman, the Spanish and the Chinese Empires on the other, war would seem positively to help mental activity. But as many examples could be found to the contrary. There may be something in the suggestion that wherever war appeared stimulating it was a war between approximate equals so that the disasters were seen to be due to human folly or perversity. In the case of the Empires, on the other hand, peace was achieved at the price of a submission to authority, bureaucratic or spiritual, which deprived men of their self-reliance and creative ability. However this may be, historical factors tend to have somewhat of a cyclic nature, and in the long run to cancel each other out, although it is always possible that one age will destroy, or cause to be forgotten, more than the previous ages produced, and that a definite culmination may be reached in human progress. This may be closer than we think (if it is not already passed) and humanity may become static until it is destroyed by cosmic forces. Yet it seems more probable that we are on the point, owing to our material achievements of reaching another order of cyclic changes, which may lead us to the stars.

Whether an age or an individual will express itself in creative thinking or in repetitive pedantry is more a matter of desire than of intellectual power, and it is probably more the nature of their desires than of their capacities that will determine whether or not humanity will develop further. Now it would seem that the present time is a very critical one for the evolution of human desire. It is an age in which the nature of desire has been glimpsed at for the first time, and that glimpse enables us to see two very different possibilities. The intellectual life, both in its scientific and its æsthetic aspects, is seen no longer as the vocation of the rational mind, but as a compensation, as a perversion of more primitive, unsatisfied desires. Now the question arises is this perversion in the line of evolution, or is it a merely temporary, pathological process? If by a sounder psychology, a way of living more in accordance with nature, it should be found that the satisfaction of purely human— or, as we might almost say, purely mammalian—desires is capable of absorbing all the energy that suppression now forces into scientific or æsthetic channels, then the human race may well find itself statically employed in leading an idyllic, Melanesian existence of eating, drinking, friendliness, love-making, dancing and singing, and the golden age may settle permanently on the world. On the other hand it may be that though the desire, the necessity to escape life on the paths of intellectual or æsthetic creation may be weakened by the application of an intelligent psychology, yet a corresponding freedom from the internal conflicts which now hinder both these forms of expression may more than compensate for what is lost, and we may find the capacity to live at the same time more fully human and fully intellectual lives. The latter alternative is more in line with the recent developments of Freudian psychology which divide the psyche into the primitive id, the ego which is its expression of contact with reality, and the super ego which represents its aspirations and ideals. Rationalism strove to make the super ego the dominant partner; it never succeeded, not only because its standard was too high to allow any outlet for the primitive forces, but because it was itself too arbitrary, too tainted with distorted primitive wishes ever to be brought into correspondence with reality. Naturalism, less definitely, aimed at giving the primitive wishes full play but equally failed because these wishes are too primitive, too infantile, too inconsistent with themselves to be satisfied even by the greatest licence. The aim of applied psychology is rather now to bring, by analysis or education, the ideals of the super ego in line with external reality, using and rendering innocuous the power of the id and leading to a life where a full adult sexuality would be balanced with objective activity. It is this alternative that makes the mechanical, biological progress that I have outlined not only possible but almost necessary, for a sound intellectual humanity will never be content with repeating itself in circles of metaphysical thinking like Shaw's Immortals, but will need a real externalization in the transforming of the universe and itself. Such a development could hardly leave unchanged the present types of human interests in art and science and religion.

It is here that prediction is most difficult and most fascinating. Under the influence of psychology it may well be that, just as all the branches of science itself are coalescing into a unified world picture, so the human activities of art and attitudes of religion may be fused into one whole action-reaction pattern of man to reality. The recognition of the art that informs all pure science need not mean the abandonment for it of all present art, rather it will mean the completion of the transformation of art that has already begun. Art expressing itself on one side in a kind of generalized architecture, massive or molecular, gives form to the infinite possibilities of the application of science; on the other a generalized poetry expresses the ever-widening complexities of the understanding of the universe, while religion clarified by psychology remains as the expression of the desire that drives man through the universe in understanding and hope.

It is not sufficient, however, to consider the absence or presence of desire for progress, because that desire itself will not make itself effective until it can overcome the quite real distaste and hatred which mechanization has already brought into being. This distaste is nothing to what the bulk of present humanity would feel about even the milder of the changes which are suggested here. The reader may have already felt that distaste, especially in relation to the bodily changes: I have felt it myself in imagining them. The effectiveness of these conservative feelings is the balance of two opposing factors. The changes in question do not come all at once: envisaged in broad outline in the sequence given, their nature would suggest that they follow each other with increasing frequency, as the past has already shown. Now the more rapid the environmental changes the less will the individual mind be able to adapt itself to them and the more violent will be its emotional reactions. At the same time these changes give more and more power to those groups of men which are involved in them and are bringing them about, so that, up to the present, in the war of the machines, the mechanists have always been the victors; but, of course, if the emotional reactions of the mass increased more rapidly than the power of the mechanists, the reverse would be the case. A severe crisis in mechanical civilization brought about by its inherent technical weakness or, as is much more likely, by its failure to arrange secondary social adjustments, is likely to be seized upon by the emotional factors hostile to all mechanism, and we may be closer to such a reversion than we suppose. Two recent books representing very divergent standpoints, the last works of Mr. Aldous Huxley and Mr. D. H. Lawrence, show at the same time the weakening desires and the imminent realization of futility on the part of the scientist, and a turning away from the whole of mechanization on the part of the more humanely-minded. The same thought is echoed from still another angle in the writings of Mr. Bertrand Russell. They may be prophets predicting truly the doom of the new Babylon or merely lamenting over a past that is lost for ever. With these uncertainties before us, each must follow his own desires, accepting that his opponent may be as right as himself. The event will show which, but only after his own time.

There remains still another possibility: the most unexpected, but not necessarily the most improbable, the development of a di-morphism in humanity in which the conflict between the humanizers and the mechanizers will be solved not by the victory of one or the other but by the splitting of the human race— the one section developing a fully-balanced humanity, the other groping unsteadily beyond it. But this possibility involves the consideration of mechanical and biological factors, the synthesis of which, with the psychological, will be attempted in my concluding pages.

V

SYNTHESIS

Having followed our main lines of change separately, it now remains for us to consider the interaction between the physical, physiological and psychological elements of future human evolution. It is very easy to see the relations of the first two: the colonization of space and the mechanization of the body are obviously complementary. The dissimilarity between the conditions of life in space and on the earth would in itself be sufficient to cause perfectly normal, unassisted, evolutionary changes in human beings, but obviously spatial conditions would be more favourable to mechanized than to organic man. If he could get rid of the major part of his body and his necessity for a relatively large intake of oxygen and water-saturated food, the cellular nature of the celestial globes would cease to be necessary. This would give mechanized man an advantage similar to that which the relatively flexible and naked animal cell has over the rigidly demarcated plant. Besides, it is only in space that the potentialities of the more highly developed forms of complex minds would have an adequate field of functioning, particularly in their extended time relations.

It may be that we are approaching or will ultimately reach a conception of time that will make transit in time as easy as transit in space. But all our present knowledge, apart from our desires, suggests that it is improbable. Even if time and space were made equivalent, to gain a second of the future would be equivalent to travelling 180,000 miles. But even without a fundamental change in the conception of time the time faculties of mechanized man would be still very different from ours. Extension will be its chief character: already in the monkey stage the actual present of an animal embraces a short part of the past and future. Anticipation of movement, through muscular innervation and memory, by its retention of nerve impulse images, extend the present to the limit of a second or so. Every time we play tennis we are prophets without knowing it of the future position of the ball which is conceived of as present. In the human stage we have extended mostly backwards as memory, our immediate prevision being limited by lack of scientific knowledge. It is now rapidly increasing, but is not usually accepted as prevision because it is conscious and intellectual. However, prevision plainly tends to become more and more deductive, and, to the mechanized man, the immediately apprehended may include years or centuries of past and future.

One may picture then, these beings, nuclearly resident, so to speak, in a relatively small set of mental units, each utilizing the bare minimum of energy, connected together by a complex of etherial intercommunication, and spreading themselves over immense areas and periods of time by means of inert sense organs which, like the field of their active operations, would be, in general, at a great distance from themselves. As the scene of life would be more the cold emptiness of space than the warm, dense atmosphere of the planets, the advantage of containing no organic material at all, so as to be independent of both of these conditions, would be increasingly felt.

It is when we turn to the interaction on the psychological plane that the difficulties again occur. The physical and the psychological have a mutual influence which it is very difficult at the present moment to estimate. Undoubtedly, if modern tendencies have any elements of permanency in them, a great deal of the activity of the future will be devoted to the end of a greater understanding of the universe. Humanity, or its descendants, may well be much more occupied with purely scientific research and much less with the necessity of satisfying primary physiological and psychological needs than it is at present. This character may stamp the whole of future development, so that machinery will be organized not for production but for discovery. Indeed, the great necessity for production either of food or other articles of consumption will disappear rapidly with the progress of dehumanization. But such changes are small compared with those which would necessarily be involved by the physiological alterations which I have suggested.

The human mind has evolved always in the company of the human body, and of the animal body before it was human. The intricate connections of mind and body must exceed our imagination, as from our point of view we are peculiarly prevented from observing them. Altering in any perfectly sound physiological or surgical way the functionings of the body will certainly have secondary but far-reaching effects on the mind, and these secondary effects are unpredictable and probably will still be unpredictable at the time when the physiological changes take place. But it is thoroughly in accord with both human and natural evolution that secondary changes should not be taken into account when reacting to the primary desire or stimulus: in other words, the physiological steps will probably be taken without consideration of the psychological consequences, which may, of course, wreck the whole organism, or, on the other hand, lead to an unpredictably large increase in mental grasp and efficiency. It is on account of this delicate balance between physiological and psychological factors that the future, as well as the present, will be full of dangerous turning-points and pitfalls. We shall have very sane reactionaries at all periods warning us to remain in the natural and primitive state of humanity, which is usually the last stage but one in their cultural history. But the secondary consequences of what men have already done—the reactionaries as much as any—will carry them away then as now. Obviously certain considerable psychological displacements or perversions must occur to balance the physiological perversions. The sexual instincts in particular, which still find considerable direct gratification, would be unrecognizably changed. One may assume that there is some kind of principle of psychological conservation which will prevent them, as it has prevented them up to the present, being suppressed altogether. But what will they be changed into? The solution may be an extension of sublimation, a process which is at present outside conscious control but which may not always remain so. A part of sexuality may go to research, and a much larger part must lead to æsthetic creation. The art of the future will, because of the very opportunities and materials it will have at its command, need an infinitely stronger formative impulse than it does now. The cardinal tendency of progress is the replacement of an indifferent chance environment by a deliberately created one. As time goes on, the acceptance, the appreciation, even the understanding of nature, will be less and less needed. In its place will come the need to determine the desirable form of the humanly-controlled universe which is nothing more nor less than art.

The psychology of a complex mind must differ almost as much from that of a simple, mechanized mind as its psychology would from ours; because something that must underlie and perhaps be even greater than sex is involved. By the intimate intercommunication of minds, the very existence of the ego would be impaired for the first time. Some kind of equilibrium will have to be found between each partial and corporate personality. This we can vaguely adumbrate when we think of the conflicts involved between ego and sexual impulses, the latter attempting always to break the isolation of the former and reach out to another individual or a group. If it is once possible to achieve this reaching out of feeling, the results are bound to be enormous and perhaps overwhelming. Will the corporate personalities form greater and greater complexes until there is only one intelligence, or will there be a multiplication of separate and differently-evolving complexes with resulting conflicts? Spatial considerations seem on the whole to favour the latter view, but we must allow for enormous increases in communications and in the capacity for rational conduct.

Another even deeper psychological consideration arises at this point. What is to be the future of feeling? Is it to be perverted or superseded altogether? In other words, are the mechanical or corporate men of the future to be emotional or rational? Here we have very little to guide us; we are not certain whether the comparative coldness of modern intellectualism is the effect of a considerable development or of dangerous repression. Even if we did know the answer to this it would hardly help us, since our new beings would have a different physiological balance. This balance will not be, as in us, at the mercy of the uncontrolled interactions of individual and environment. Feeling, or at any rate, feeling-tones, will almost certainly be under conscious control: a feeling-tone will be induced in order to favour the performance of a particular kind of operation. Of course, it would be excessively dangerous for human beings in their present state to have this control of their feelings. A great majority would probably be content to remain in a state of more or less ecstatic happiness, but the man of the future will probably have discovered that happiness is not an end of life. This is as far as we may go even in guessing. The psychology of the completely mechanized organism must remain a mystery.

Viewed from the standpoint of the present the carrying out of such a programme of human development must seem a very pointless occupation; but it is doubtful whether the present civilization would appear to an educated Athenean as something worthy to mark the culmination of his efforts. We must not assume static psychology and a further static knowledge. The immediate future which is our own desire, we seek; in achieving it we become different; becoming different we desire something new, so there is no staleness except when development itself has stopped. Moreover, development, even in the most refined stages, will always be a very critical process; the dangers to the whole structure of humanity and its successors will not decrease as their wisdom increases, because, knowing more and wanting more they will dare more, and in daring will risk their own destruction. But this daring, this experimentation, is really the essential quality of life.

V I

POSSIBILITY

By now it should be possible to make a picture of the general scheme of development as a unified whole, and though each part may seem plausible in detail, yet in some obscure way the total result seems unbelievable. This disbelief may be well founded, for what is suggested is not so much a fulfilling as a transformation of humanity, a setting up of what is virtually a new species or several new species, and a mode of setting up which is in itself a departure from the time-hallowed methods of evolution. Now, I believe, that this scheme is more than a bare possibility, that it, or something like it, has about an even chance of occurring; but I must justify this belief not by hypothetics of the future but by analysis of causes acting in the present. Perhaps the most fruitful way of beginning is to ask the question, "What is the effective purpose of the human race as it now is?" We can eliminate such satisfactory answers as "For the glory of God," because, however true, they do not differentiate humanity from other parts of creation. The answer one seeks is the historical and economic one. Human societies are recent products and, up to the present, can be essentially qualified as co-operative food-producing societies— or perhaps, to include comfort, as co-operative body-satisfying societies. They are distinguished in this way from insect societies, which are essentially, as Wheeler has pointed out, reproductive societies. True, in fulfilling the function of securing a brood, insect societies have gone far in becoming food-producing units, and the complementary process in man is shown by the increased care taken over education; but devotion to children has never been the mainspring of human activity. Hunger and sex still dominate the primitive mammalian side of human existence, but at the present time it looks as if humanity were within sight of their satisfaction. Permanent plenty, no longer a Utopian dream, awaits the arrival of permanent peace. Even now, through rationalized capitalism or Soviet state planning, the problem of the production and distribution of necessaries to the primary satisfaction of all human beings, is being pushed forward with uniform and intelligent method. Stupidity and the perversity of separate interests may hold the consummation back for centuries, but it must come gradually and surely.

Now supposing this state achieved or approximating to achievement, what is to become of humanity? Is it, like the stabilized insect societies, to settle down to an eternity of methodical enjoyment, or is there appearing, by some unforeseen chance, a new objective, a new reason for existing beyond the calls of hunger and lust? The primates, and subsequently man, developed intelligence in order to satisfy their desires in a world that was getting more and more difficult to live in. They developed it as primitive plants develop the habit of eating, or fish that of breathing, and just as those plants became animals who lived to eat and those fish became animals that lived to breathe, so we may, in time, come to live to think instead of thinking to live. But this biological analogy carries a very suggestive element; more fish remain in the sea than ever came out of it. It is not the habit of evolutionary processes to transform the whole of one state of living into another. Rather does nature pick some particularly happy development and allow it to expand in the place of and even at the expense of her earlier efforts. If man is to develop something new, the insistent question is, whether all humanity is going to develop or only a part of it? The biological analogy in favour of the latter would be overwhelming if man were an ordinary species, but it happens that at the moment, for the first time in his history, he consists virtually of one society, and we have no precedent for the development of any new types, particularly of solitary types, from the middle of a single society; but what, of course, could develop from a society would be another society, at first simply a part of it, but afterwards differentiating itself more and more clearly.

If we consider only those alternatives that lead to development, leaving on one side the not impossible state in which mankind would be stabilized and live an oscillating existence for millennia, we have to consider, in the light of the present, the alternatives: whether mankind will progress as a whole or will divide definitely into a progressive and unprogressive part. Over and over again in history there has occurred the raising of a particular class or a particular culture to a point at which there seemed a permanent gulf between it and other cultures or classes. Yet the gulf was not permanent; the particular aristocracy fell or its advantages spread themselves so widely that they became common stock. The cause for this is not obscure: first, the aristocrats differed only superficially from the many, and secondly they were not progressing themselves in such a way as to increase their distance and leave humanity behind. The present aristocracy of western culture, at the very moment when it most clearly dominates the world, is being imitated rapidly and successfully in every eastern country. It is not on the lines of a cultural aristocracy or the formation of a class more able to lead the good life that the splitting of the human race is likely to occur; because such aristocracies are only reaching to a more complete humanity, and where they lead the race will follow. It is rather the aristocracy of scientific intelligence that may give rise to new developments. They have come down the earlier centuries, scattered singly or in small groups, but the mechanical revolution and its consequences have increased their number and at the same time their compactness. More and more, the world may be run by the scientific expert. The new nations, America, China and Russia, have begun to adapt to this idea consciously. Scientific bodies naturally are first conceived of as advisory and they will probably never become anything else; but, with every advance in the direction of more rational psychology, the power of advice will increase and that of force proportionately decrease. This development, coupled with the broadening of the idea of private interest to include, almost necessarily, some consideration of humanity, will tend to centre real sovereignty in advisory bodies. The scientists would then have a dual function: to keep the world going as an efficient food and comfort machine, and to worry out the secrets of nature for themselves. It may well be that the dreams of "Dædalus" and the doom of "Icarus" may both be fulfilled. A happy prosperous humanity enjoying their bodies, exercising the arts, patronizing the religions, may be well content to leave the machine, by which their desires are satisfied, in other and more efficient hands. Psychological and physiological discoveries will give the ruling powers the means of directing the masses in harmless occupations and of maintaining a perfect docility under the appearance of perfect freedom. But this cannot happen unless the ruling powers are the scientists themselves. For a state in which the present rulers impose themselves in this way, the prospect of which so appals Mr. Bertrand Russell, though possible, is essentially unstable and bound to lead to revolution, which would be brought about by the gradually increasing inefficiency of the rulers and the increasingly effective insurgence of the excluded intelligent. Even a scientific state could only maintain itself by perpetually increasing its power over the non-living and living environment. If it failed to do so, it would relapse into pedantry and become a perfectly ordinary aristocracy. In the earlier chapters I have given some idea of one way in which this scientific development could take place by the colonization of the universe and the mechanization of the human body. Once this process had started, particularly on the physiological side, there would be an effective bar between the altered and the non-altered humanity. The separation of the scientists and those who thought like them—a class of technicians and experts who would perhaps form ten per cent. or so of the world's population—from the rest of humanity, would save the struggle and difficulty which would be bound to ensue if there were any attempt to change the whole bulk of the population, and would, to a certain extent, lessen the hostility that these fundamental changes would necessarily produce. Mankind as a whole given peace, plenty and freedom, might well be content to let alone the fanatical but useful people who chose to distort their bodies or blow themselves into space; and if, at some time, the magnitude of the changes made them aware that something important and terrifying had happened, it would then be too late for them to do anything about it. Even if a wave to primitive obscurantism then swept the world clear of the heresy of science, science would already be on its way to the stars.

In tracing this development, however, we have

neglected other weighty considerations. Up to the present the cumulative edifice of science has been erected by assistance as much from the practical world as from the learned, and scientists themselves have never formed an hereditary or even a closed caste. In two ways the progress of science depends upon non-scientific humanity. As experimentation becomes more complex, the need for the co-operation in it of technical elements from outside becomes greater and the modern laboratory tends increasingly to resemble the factory and to employ in its service increasing numbers of purely routine workers. If development is to follow, even in the earliest stages, on the lines I have indicated above, this necessity for economic and technical assistance will be multiplied many times. More important still, the complexities of scientific—and particularly of theoretical scientific —thought, calls for an ever greater number of first-class intelligences, and the modern development of science can hardly be disconnected from the political and economic changes which make it possible to recruit the personnel of science from wider and wider circles. For until we can know from the inspection of an infant or an ovum that it will develop into a genius, or else can from any infant produce one by a suitable education we shall have to rely on the diffusion of a general education in order to ensure that all capable minds are utilized.

This recruiting of science is the surest way of preventing a permanent human di-morphism from arising, because it reinforces what is probably the strongest factor involved, the emotional conservatism of the scientist themselves. The mere observation of scientists should be sufficient at the present to show that any fear of immediate di-morphism is unfounded. In every respect, save their work, they resemble their non-scientific brothers, and no one would be more shocked than they at the suggestion that they were raising up a new species and abandoning the bulk of mankind. For whether they are inventing submarines or depth charges, they feel they are serving humanity. The consciousness of solidarity— and even more, the unconscious emotional identification with the group—is a terrific force binding humanity together, and so long as individual scientists have it, di-morphism would be impossible.

But the scientists are not masters of the destiny of science; the changes they bring about may, without their knowing it, force them into positions which they would never have chosen. Their curiosity and its effects may be stronger than their humanity.

These two obstacles to the separation of the

scientists, though weighty, are of the kind that would lose force with time, while those favouring their separation tend to increase. The technical importance of the scientist is bound to give him the independent administration of large funds and end the mendicant state in which he exists at present. Scientific corporations might well become almost independent states and be enabled to undertake their largest experiments without consulting the outside world—a world which would be less and less able to judge what the experiments were about. It is very probable that before the real independence of science could make itself felt, the organization of the world would have to pass through its present semi-capitalistic stage to complete proletarian dictatorship, because it is unlikely that a scientific corporation would, in an ordinary capitalistic state, be allowed to be so wealthy and powerful. In a Soviet state (not the state of the present, but one freed from the danger of capitalist attack), the scientific institutions would in fact gradually become the government, and a further stage of the Marxian hierarchy of domination would be reached. Scientists in such a stage would tend very naturally to identify themselves emotionally rather with the progress of science itself than with that of a class, a nation or a humanity outside science, while the rest of the population would, by the diffusion of

an education in which the highest values lay in a
scientific rather than in a moral or a political direction, be much less likely to oppose effectively the development of science. Thus the balance which is now
against the splitting of mankind might well turn,
almost imperceptibly, in the opposite direction. The
whole question is one largely of numbers, and would
become entirely so as soon as the quantity and quality
of population were controlled by authority. From one
point of view the scientists would emerge as a new
species and leave humanity behind; from another,
humanity—the humanity that counts—might seem to
change *en bloc*, leaving behind in a relatively primitive state those too stupid or too stubborn to change.
The latter view suggests another biological analogy:
there may not be room for both types in the same
world and the old mechanism of extinction will come
into play. The better organized beings will be obliged
in self-defence to reduce the numbers of the others,
until they are no longer seriously inconvenienced by
them. If, as we may well suppose, the colonization of
space will have taken place or be taking place while
these changes are occurring, it may offer a very convenient solution. Mankind—the old mankind—would
be left in undisputed possession of the earth, to be
regarded by the inhabitants of the celestial spheres
with a curious reverence. The world might, in fact,

be transformed into a human zoo, a zoo so intelligently managed that its inhabitants are not aware that they are there merely for the purposes of observation and experiment.

That prospect should please both sides: it should satisfy the scientists in their aspirations towards further knowledge and further experience, and the humanists in their looking for the good life on earth. But somehow it fails by the very virtue of its being a possible and probable solution on the lines of our own knowledge. We do not really expect or want the probable; all, even the least religious, retain in their minds when they think of the future, an idea of the *deus ex machina*, of some transcendental, superhuman event which will, without their help, bring the universe to perfection or destruction. We want the future to be mysterious and full of supernatural power; and yet these very aspirations, so totally removed from the physical world, have built this material civilization and will go on building it into the future so long as there remains any relation between aspiration and action. But can we count on this? Or, rather, have we not here the criterion which will decide the direction of human development? We are on the point of being able to see the effects of our actions and their probable consequences in the future; we hold the future still timidly, but perceive it for the first time, as a function of our own action. Having seen it, are we to turn away from something that offends the very nature of our earliest desires, or is the recognition of our new powers sufficient to change those desires into the service of the future which they will have to bring about?

A NOTE ON THE TYPE

The text of this book was set on the Linotype in a face called MONTICELLO. This type, issued by The Mergenthaler Linotype Company in 1950 is based on a cutting called "Ronaldson Roman No. 1," a late eighteenth-century production of the Binny & Ronaldson foundry of Philadelphia. Monticello belongs to the family of transitional faces which includes Bell Roman, Baskerville, Bulmer and Fournier. The Transitionals fall between the hearty "Old Style" taste represented by Caslon's letters, and the graver-styled nineteenth-century "Moderns."

The book was printed and bound by The Haddon Craftsmen, Scranton, Pa. Paper was manufactured by P. H. Glatfelter, Spring Grove, Pa. Design by Guy Fleming.